From Employee to Employer in 30 Days

Repeatable Tips on How to Build a Business That Attracts Profits Almost Immediately

By: Donna Nelson

9781635014426

PUBLISHERS NOTES

Disclaimer – Speedy Publishing LLC

Speedy Publishing LLC

40 E Main Street, Newark, Delaware, 19711

Contact Us: 1-888-248-4521

Website: http://www.speedypublishing.co

REPRINTED Paperback Edition: 9781635014426:

Manufactured in the United States of America

DEDICATION

This book is dedicated to Stefan. Though worlds apart, you will always be in my heart. Thank you for the inspiration and for constantly challenging me to do better at everything I do.

TABLE OF CONTENTS

CHAPTER 1- WANTED FOR BUSINESS: LEADERS

A great business leader is a many-sided person who has a lot of strengths and capabilities. He may manage budgets, spearhead marketing campaigns, plan products, network with industry experts, and assess contract management software. He's dedicated, industrious, bright, and creative. However, even with all these admonitory qualities, a business leader is really only a leader if he likewise has one crucial trait: motivation skills.

As a matter of fact, regardless of your walk of life, if you seek to be a successful leader you have to be able to motivate the individuals who follow your guidance. Motivated people are more productive and cohesive. They likewise are more likely to be pleased with their job and less likely to look for work elsewhere. However how may you motivate your people and accomplish these results? How may you make them as passionate about your business as you are? Here are a few hints:

There are 2 general ways of expressly motivating individuals: positive bonuses and negative tactics. Utilizing positive motivation produces goals and incentives to which your people may strive. Negative motivation involves utilizing threats or fear of reprisal in order to accomplish productivity goals. Far too many people utilize a combination of the 2 in their attempt to motivate; this approach causes threats and incentives to cancel one another out and bring about counterproductive ends. For this reason it's crucial to have a clear approach.

Naturally, when deciding between the 2, most experts would say that positive motivation nearly always works best. Along similar lines, motivation frequently rises when a collaborative work environment is furthered. While producing individualized incentives might breed stress and competition among people, group projects and targets may transform into productivity, cohesion, and more propelled people, even on an individual level. Bear in mind that a desire to construct a team culture ought to carry over into other areas. People who are good fit for the business ought to be sought out. People who detract from it, conversely, ought to probably be let go.

Hopefully these tips may help you plan a suitable motivational approach. While a good business leader might be highly motivated, a great one needs to be just as capable of instilling that same spirit in his people.

Donna Nelson
What Makes a Brand Successful?

The opening move to building a successful brand is to set a clear-cut brand vision and set of objectives, which ought to be aimed at the following criteria for a successful brand.

1. Distinction

Your brand has to be different, if you provide the same value at the same price why would a consumer select you over your established rival? Your brand has to clearly convey this.

2. Added worth

Your brand has to add extra value to the buyer. 'Me too' products are all right as part of an extended product portfolio, however if your buyers are to part with their money, they require added value and this ought to extend right through to the entire product level e.g. to include services.

3. Quality

If your brand and products are of inferior quality, you are able to forget brand allegiance. Regrettably there are a number of rivals waiting to take your market share, and brand allegiance is becoming less common as rivals utilize all sorts of tricks to win over your buyers; don't let pitiful quality be a reason for lost business.

4. Structured communications

With markets getting saturated, being memorable for the correct reasons is central to any brand's success. Your promotional technique has to be tight, sending one marketing e-mail a month isn't adequate; you need an intermingled, 'through the line' communications technique which keeps the momentum of your brand.

5.Direction and support

Individuals are the key to your business and internal marketing ought to be a top precedence for any marketing manager. You are able to spend 10's of thousands on your brand all to be forgotten when a buyer pops up and your people haven't heard of the deal or offer! Invest time and cash in internal marketing and ensure you've a strong set of brand guidelines to support your people.

6.Originality

Innovation is more than simply a thought; it's about innovating products, procedures, structure and your brand! Your buyers' needs are always shifting and your brand must respond to this; the product life cycle is a denotation that it won't sell forever, so keep your brand running. I think there's one key point missing here and that's producing an emotional connection with your buyers.

CHAPTER 2- STARTING A PROFITABLE BUSINESS WITH AN EFFECTIVE PLAN

You're ready to create your business plan... or are you? Here are the basics you need to have in place.

Step 1. Define Your Business

You have a good idea of what you want your business to do. You've done preliminary research and identified your target market. You know what type of business model you want; whether it's retail or trade, service-based or product based. So how would you explain your business, if asked to do so? Many people find themselves hemming and hawing at this point. You know what it's all about, but it's a little hard to sum up. If this sounds like you, you're not ready to sit down and put your plan together. You need to define your business model the way a diamond cutter perfects a diamond.

From Employee to Employer in 30 Days
Ask yourself the following questions:

•What does my business do?

•How does it do it?

•Who does it serve?

•What "gap" does it fill?

•What is unique and special about my business?

•What is my business' strongest advantage for its clients or customers?

It may be a trifle outmoded, but after you've done this, think "elevator speech". Imagine stepping into an elevator and bumping into someone who asks you what your business is all about. What would you answer, in three lines or less? How would you strip away all irrelevant detail? How would you summarize your business?

Step 2. Write your Mission Statement

One of the best ways to create your elevator speech lies in writing out a mission statement for your business. This doesn't just explain what it sells or what it does: It encapsulates your company's core values, beliefs, ethics, goals and purpose. The best way start writing: Look at examples of other company mission statements. These can be as short as a simple sentence, tag line or slogan... or comprise more than one paragraph: However, mission statements should try to get to the heart of your business as clearly and directly as possible.

Donna Nelson

Let's take a quick look at a sampling of effective Fortune 500 company mission statements:

- "To make the world's information universally accessible and useful" – Google

- "To be America's best run, most profitable automotive retailer" – AutoNation, Fort Lauderdale, FLA

- "To discover, develop and deliver innovative medicines that help patients prevail over serious diseases" – Bristol-Myers Squibb Company, New York, NY

- "Create value for shareholders through the energy business" – Kerr-McGee Corporation, Oklahoma City, OK

- "Mattel makes a difference in the global community by effectively serving children in need. Partnering with charitable organizations dedicated to directly serving children, Mattel creates joy through the Mattel Children's Foundation, product donations, grant making and the work of employee volunteers. We also enrich the lives of Mattel employees by identifying diverse volunteer opportunities and supporting their personal contributions through the matching gifts program."

- "To bring inspiration and innovation to every athlete in the world" – Nike Inc., Beaverton, OR

- "Our business is pharmaceutical care. Our mission is positive outcomes" – OmniCare, Covington, KY

- "We fear change." – Wayne Campbell, Wayne's World, movie; 1992

When writing your company mission statement, follow these tips:

1. Be as clear and direct as possible

2. Avoid clichés and overused phrases like "culture of diversity" or "with particular emphasis on"

3. Cut out adjectives and adverbs, which weaken your prose. If a sentence doesn't work without adjectives and adverbs, split it into shorter sentences and rewrite completely

4. Cut out unnecessary words. This includes filler phrases such as "Be that as it may" and "unlikely though it may be".

5. Show how your company benefits the community, shareholders and/or the world. You may find yourself amazed at how much writing a strong mission statement clarifies your company vision. (Keep it short enough and it can double as your slogan or tag line – and help brand your business – just as DeBeers did with its famous slogan, below.)

Step 3. Decide Which Type of Plan You Need

Who is it for? What effect does it have to have on them? Do you need to provide projections for a Feasibility study? Are you attempting to show how financing would bring a successful return to a bank or investor? Decide which of the following plan types will best serve your purpose at this time.

•Start-up Plan – For your own clarification; or for presenting to potential investors or backers

•Feasibility Study – As above; plus more in-depth market analysis and projected costs and expenses

- Strategic Plan – Strictly internal; all about actions that need to be taken. May be included in a company manual

- Operations Plan – Annual road map containing implementation dates, deadlines and responsibility allocation

- Internal Plan – Overview or snapshot, to be included in the company manual

- Expansion Plan – Similar to a Feasibility Study. Detailed report aimed at investors, banks and backers. Includes profits and losses, projected growth and expenses, opportunities and steps for expansion

Step 4. Assembling Your Data

Make sure you have all the data and research you need completed and at hand. This can include:

- Survey results, scans and screenshots

- Industry statistics

- Statistics from any split-testing you may have done

- Market research results

- Sales figures

- A balance sheet

- Other financial data

- Your mission statement, slogan and/or tagline

•Graphic files containing your company logo, in .JPG or .PNG format

•Headshot .JPG or .PNG

•Any other relevant photographs in .JPG or .PNG file, including a snapshot of your premises; headshots for any key personnel or staff members

Step 5. Use a Template

If you've never created a Business Plan before, your best bet is to use a template. You can either obtain a sample of an existing plan (online or from your bookkeeper or a friend with a successful business) then model your own on that one or you can download an actual blank template (recommended).

If you want a free template, you can easily use MS Word to help you search Office.com for likely candidates. If you have MS Word 2010, simply click on your "File" tab, then "New" in the left-hand, vertical menu. Overwrite "Search Office.com for templates" with "Business Plan". Browse through available plans, and select the best candidate; then press the "Download" button. (Be sure to save a Master Copy of your new Template!) Not all these templates are created equal, so do pay attention to the rating given each one in the right-hand sidebar.

Step 6. Start Writing!

Once you've assembled your data, create an outline before you ever enter a word of body text. This will help you create a well-balanced plan that is neither missing any sections nor focusing too much on one particular section. If you are using a Template that already provides you with a structured table of contents and outline, you can simply start filling in your body data straight away. Ditto, if you are using an online wizard.

If you are writing from scratch, however, it is vital to create your outline first. In any type of business plan, your headings should include:

• A cover page, with your logo and who the Plan is for

• A Table of Contents (TOC)

• A Mission Statement

• Executive Summary (if applicable). After that, add or include sections as needed, depending on the type of plan you intend to create.

A basic Start-up Plan or Feasibility Study should contain (after the previous sections already indicated) a TOC sectioned into the following basic sections:

1. Market Customer

a. Profile Competition

b. Market Size and Market Share

2. Marketing Plan

a. Pricing Location,

b. Place or Distribution/Delivery

c. Manufacturing Process (if applicable)

3.One to Three Year Financial Projections

a.Startup Costs

b.Sales Forecast

The amount of detail in each section will depend on the type of plan.

Step 7. Proof Your Plan

When you have finished your business plan, run a spell checker on it. Go through the results carefully and make any corrections. Then save your plan, and put it away for at least a day. Next morning, read through it. Correct any errors and highlight klutzy sentences you want to rework. Run the spell checker again. Let it sit. Re-read it and proof it again.

Create a Master Copy and backup in both digital and print format before distributing printouts of your plan to the proper parties. Congratulations – you have now completed your first business plan. Just remember that business flans are never static: They are living, breathing roadmaps for your growing – and successful – business.

CHAPTER 3- A TEAM PLAYER IS A PERFECT BUSINESS LEADER

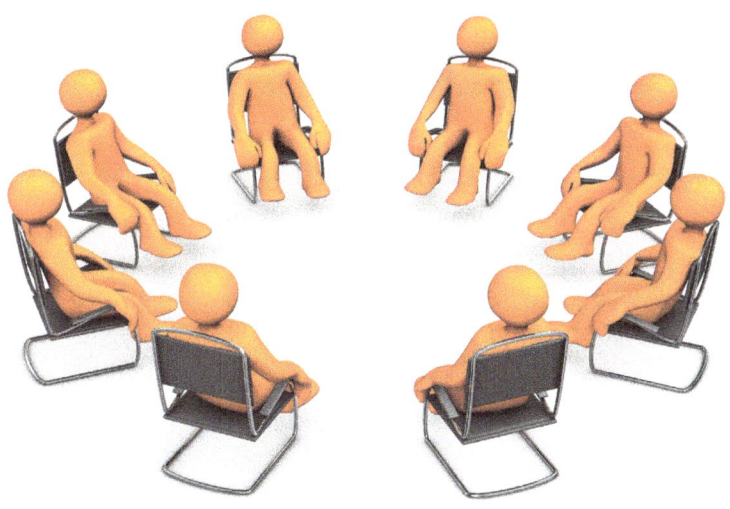

The team members in the team ought to be aware of what is happening in reference to anything affecting the team. If anything of importance is materializing, everyone in the team ought to be made aware of the occurrence and how it's going to affect the team.

The members of the team and the team leaders should have beneficial communication and be open at all times. Such open communicating is essential to build rapport among team members and for the evolution of trust.

All the team members ought to be made aware of their duties towards the project. They ought to be apportioned truthful goals and be made to accomplish them with ease. Any help that's needed toward completion of their responsibilities ought to be supplied when demanded. The team leader ought to work hand in hand with the team members with beneficial time management and participation. Such participations won't only assist in getting the job accomplished effectively, the team leader will also know the advancement of the project firsthand and this will likewise help build great rapport and trust.

However, at the same time, the team leader shouldn't butt into the functions being accomplished by the other team members as this will lead to friction and bitterness. As much independence in making decisions ought to be furnished with enough support from the periphery. The project will be a job that's achieved by the climax of the efforts of all the members of the team. This is like matching all the pieces of a puzzle to produce a big picture. In order to accomplish this, the parts ought to be properly matched in the correct place. If one isn't correct the picture won't turn out right. For this reason, there should be a beneficial action design in place for the team to work in tandem and achieve the project cleanly.

The team leader shouldn't be dominating over the other members of the team. Everyone ought to be an equal participant in the project and have their say in the preparation of plans. However, it ought to be the leader's last say in deciding the course of action after carefully hashing it out with all the team members. Team building ought to be a cautiously figured process and these self-improvement tips ought to help. If attempts are taken to arrange the correct team and the team is worked at an individual level and collective level, it might run well as a group and the joint attempts may be utilized to execute the required jobs without a great deal of issues.

Are You Driven and Motivated Enough?

Failure might sometimes be the reason why individuals change. Receiving failed grades make us recognize that we need to study.

Debts remind us of our inability to look for a source of money. Getting humiliated gives us the 'push' to speak up and fight for ourselves to save our face from the next embarrassments. It might be a bitter experience, a friend's tragic story, a good movie, or an inspiring book that will help us get up and acquire just the right amount of motivation we need in order to better ourselves and our business.

With the infinite negativities the world brings about, how do we keep motivated?

• Accomplish your aspirations. Avoid negative individuals, things and places. Roosevelt once said, "The future belongs to those who trust in the beauty of their aspirations."

• Trust in yourself, and in what you can accomplish.

• Think about things on every angle and aspect. Motivation derives from determination. To be able to understand life, you ought to feel the sun from both sides.

• Don't quit and don't give in.

• Enjoy. Work as though you don't need cash. Dance as if nobody's looking on. Love as though you never cried. Learn like you'll live forever. Motivation takes place if individuals are happy.

• Loved ones and Friends – are life's greatest treasures. Don't lose sight of them.

• Give more. Where does motivation and self-reformation take place at work, at home, and at school if you exert additional effort in doing things.

- Hold on to your aspirations. They might dangle in there for a bit, but these little stars will be your drive.

- Dismiss those who attempt to destroy you. Don't let other individuals to get the best of you. Stay away from toxic individuals – the sort of friends who hate to hear about your success.

- Simply be yourself. The key to success is to be you. And the key to failure is to attempt to please everybody.

- Continue trying no matter how difficult life might seem. If a person is motivated, sooner or later he sees a harsh life finally clearing out, paving the way to self-improvement.

- Never lie, cheat or steal. Always play a fair game.

- Practice makes perfect. Practice is about motivation. It lets us learn repertoire and ways on how can we recover from our errors.

- Ready yourself. Motivation is likewise about preparation. Stop procrastinating.

- Understand other people. If you know very well how to talk, you ought to also learn how to listen. Understand first, and to be understood the second.

- Visualize it. Motivation without vision is like a boat on land.

- Want it more than anything. Dreaming means believing.

- Zero in on your aspirations and go for it!!!

CHAPTER 4- IMPROVE ON YOUR MARKETING EVERY DAY

Top sales pros affirm that it a great deal of the time takes seven or more communications or sales messages before prospective buyers make a purchase. They in addition to that confirm that it's normally easier to sell to a referral, because somebody they know gave favorable testimonial about their products or services. What would come about if you combined both of these potent ideas? A nifty and thrifty two-step.

Check out this two-step tip:

1. Accumulate leads with your auto responder. Ask for mailing addresses and phone numbers, too, for additional ways to follow up with each individual. When you download the e-mail digest of everyone's e-mail addresses and additional information from those who asked for additional information from your auto responder, follow up multiple ways. Send out postcards. Call, mail or e-mail sales letters and additional promotional pieces.

2. Release a price list of all the products and services that you provide in an insert, direct marketing package and / or .pdf to be made available thru your auto responder. You might likewise include order forms, product descriptions, and additional sales material. Then send to the individuals in #1 above with monthly updates, announcements of recent sales and products / services, and a request for referrals.

So why not improve your closing ratio and reach out even farther at the same time? Do the two-step!

Your Relationship With Other People Counts

Ideally, when you perform buyer service, it's done on a one-on-one basis with each of your customers. That works quite well in the offline world – but on the Net, that simply won't do. Your customers are literally all over the Earth, and there's no way that you can truly deal with each one of them in person. That's where an autoresponder comes in.

Buyer service with autoresponders is quite easy. When an order is placed, an autoresponder may send out the receipt for the sale, the info for accessing the product, and a 'thank you' e-mail. This occurs whether you're logged in to your computer or on vacation in an exotic location! However customer service doesn't always end right there, and if you're away from your PC, you might be letting your buyers down! For example, an elderly gentleman sees your product advertised and places an order.

Everything runs through just fine, and he receives the receipt, the download info, and your 'thank you' e-mail. Your product is an eBook, compiled into a PDF file. This certain gentleman doesn't understand what a PDF file is, and he has no clue what you mean by 'right click to download.' He needs additional buyer service for the product that he has bought, and there's nobody available to help him – nobody but an autoresponder.

Arrange an additional autoresponder that will send a list of frequently asked questions or issues that deal with buyer service or how to access the product. Likewise arrange a support autoresponder. If he sends off a message to support, he ought to get an instant message back letting him know that his message has been received, and how shortly it will be addressed. This will supply him some measure of solace, and in most cases, he will wait that assigned time period for assistance. All the same, if he doesn't know how to download the product, and he sends off a message to support, and nothing occurs, he will most likely get very dissatisfied in a very short time period.

The difference between a patient buyer and an irate buyer is one simple autoresponder message that can and should be set up in under 5 minutes. Truly think your ordering process through, and consider the potential issues that might occur for your buyers. Get an autoresponder set up to address those issues and you'll find that your purchasers are more satisfied with your products, and exceedingly satisfied with your buyer service – all because your autoresponders handle their Issues immediately!

Other Useful Marketing Strategies

1.Surveys

Create a survey to find out what motivates your customers to buy and have questions whose answers will tell you where and how to reach your target market. Do remember to offer a gift or discount for completing your survey.

2.Free information / factsheet

Use a two-step approach to increase conversions. First, offer free business related information to potential customers that showcases your expertise. Add these potentials into your mailing list and build a relationship with them by connecting with them often.

3.Partnerships

By teaming up with another business which is related to your product, advertising costs can be shared with that company so that you can print high-quality and larger ads more affordably. Companies that have products which complement yours are potentially great partners to work with.

4. Commitment and consistency

Studies showed that a repeated message is often well remembered. Commit to consistently send mailers to the same group of people in your target market. For advertising, do it whenever affordable.

5.Increase Pricing

People often associate premium products with higher prices therefore, it is advisable to raise your prices because that separates you from the crowd and implies that your product is better and deserves the premium price. However, do take special care that the customer must see the value of the higher price.

6. Credibility of trends and current events

Consider tying your product or service with trends or current events because this allows you to gain valuable credibility and interest by association with popular groups.

7. Limited Time Only

Use time limits on your offers and promotional materials. This is to encourage action to be taken by your potential customers.

8. Fear or pain of loss

The fear or pain of loss is a very powerful sales-boosting tool. Emotions such as these can be stimulated by products that increase personal security, personal safety, personal safety or health. Make your potential customers feel that if they don't get your product or service now, they will miss out on something.

9. Long term advertisements

If you are buying advertisements, buy those that last for months. Some examples include, magnetic signs for cars or vans, car decals, putting signs on truck tailgates and rear windows, stickers on T-shirts, design the outside of the brochure to be permanent and the inside for future changes etc.

10.   Be grateful

People remember your kindness. There are many things you can be grateful about, someone who refers business to you, reliable suppliers etc. You can thank people with a special offer; make a personalized thank you card, phone call, discounts, flowers, dinner or even a commission.

11.   Business Cards for All Employees

Your employees will be proud to leave the business cards you print for them customized with their names with every customer and every prospect. They may even pass cards to their friends and relatives and your name will be in many more places.

12.   Follow the successful

Identify the winners in your industry and analyze their marketing strategies. Pick out the ones that you can use to improve on them and adapt them to your own business.

13.   Organize Parties / Events

Send out party invitations to clients and friends and plan an event to demonstrate your product or service. Make the buying process easier for your customers by eliminating all the long complicated payment methods. Let the media know about that you are unveiling interesting new products.

14.   Sincerity

People can feel it when you want to sell them something and that is an uncomfortable feeling. Genuinely offer customers useful products and services that make you and them happy. Follow your passion, do what you love and the money will follow.

15.   Set up an advisory board

For a business to grow, you need honest feedback from people you can trust. Some of the feedback may be harsh but this is a good thing because you can take those opinions and work on improving your business. Get these people (friends, family, business associates whose opinions and judgment you value) to critique every aspect of your business so that you can get a different look at your business.

16.   Use a Dipstick Now And Then

When explaining your product or service to potential clients, pause every now and then to ask questions. This is to check whether your explanation has been received by the other party. You can't sell your product or service if your message is not being received.

17.   Never Assume

Assumptions are often stumbling blocks even before you present your product or service to a potential client. It often stems from you not having the confidence in your product or service. Have a strong belief in your business and the need it fills.

18.   A bite at a time

How do you eat an elephant? A bite at a time. Reputable and successful companies did not start out exploding millions of dollars in profit, they started out small. So continue to stay focused and determined about the success of your company even though you are not at the pinnacle of success yet.

19.   Public Library

The library has a comprehensive collection of business books. Although their list is not exhaustive, at least you have got somewhere to start if you needed to learn something that can help you in your business. You can also save time in research because you can ask librarians for the information you need and they will find it for you. Not all the books you loaned are suitable for your business. Read over the books and then select and buy the ones you want to add to your own business library.

20.   Use One Media to Direct Your Customer to Another

If your target market research told you that the most popular channel to reach your target audience is through one media but your product or service works better on another media channel, use the media popular to your target market to direct your potential clients to the other media channel that is more effective in sending the message of your product or service.

21.   Invite Complaints about Your Business or Product

This point concerns after-purchase customer service. Call your customers after the sale is made or send them a post card to ask how is the performance of your product or quality of your service. If there was any problem, at least you can rectify it with immediate promptness, rather than hearing the complaint from other channels.

22.   Sloppy success is better than perfect mediocrity

Your communications materials will never be 100% perfect. It can always be improved on or revised. There's a saying that goes "Sloppy success is better than perfect mediocrity". When you have a product that can save the world, it is more important to get the message out there as fast as you can. The more you delay, the more chances you are providing for fellow competitors to latch on your idea and reach your customers faster than you can.

Donna Nelson
23.   Swipe Files

Collect and compile a list of good ads and brochures into a swipe. Use this file as a form of inspiration when you experience a creative block when designing your own advertising. Don't copy them entirely but adapt the use of it to your own business.

24.   Put yourself in your customers' shoes

Don't assume something to be important to you works the same for your customers. Always put yourself in your customers' shoes and look at it from your customers' point of view, not the company's. The rule is "take care of the customer and he'll take care of the company".

25.   Go the extra mile - give your customers more than they expected

Go the extra mile to surprise your customers with more value beyond what your product or service offers.

26.   Talk to suppliers and vendors

Get competitor information from your suppliers and vendors. By building a relationship with them, they might, unknowingly, give you crucial information about your competitors' future plans through casual talk. Alternatively, you can buy the stocks of your competitor's company if it is public-listed. As a stockholder you will receive all their annual and quarterly reports.

27.   Know the demographics of your sales area

Knowing the demographics of your target audience is important because only then will you get ideas about how to market your product or service to them. You can get such information from local newspapers by asking them for an advertising rate kit. Some other places you can research are the local chamber of commerce, the city planning commission, the public library or local TV and radio stations.

28.   Subscribe to industry magazines

Get a list of magazines from your public library. Subscribing to trade magazines related to your industry help you keep up with what's happening in your industry.

29.   Subscribe to magazines that help your business self-esteem

Immerse yourself with positive business messages by subscribing to magazines that help build your business self-esteem. Read the success stories of entrepreneurs and business people.

30.   Join organizations that can help you

Join organizations that support your industry. You can find the list of such organizations at your local public library or online. Go for conventions organized by those organizations and network with the people who are in the same industry as you to exchange business promotion and marketing ideas or strategies. There is always someone at these meetings who can help you succeed.

31.   Matching a competitor's offer

Offer a better deal for a shorter time. Limit your irresistible offer and you will still drain off a lot of his customers on a busy sale day and you will be perceived as a better place to do business.

32.   Have the knowledge of your clients' special needs at your fingertips

Have a spreadsheet to keep track of clients' requests for special services and products and whether you can meet these requests. With this information, you can track interest in new products or services that you should offer.

33.   Be reachable

Be sure to include you contact details on every single communications collateral your company sends out so that customers can easily search for your contact when they need to. You can print your company name, address, and fax number on all materials including, packing slips and invoices.

34.   Use personalized post-it notes to promote your company

Design and create personalized post-it notepads to promote your company. Every office uses post-its and they stick them to everything. Due to the fact that they use your post-its every day, it is the case of repeated advertising. If they have a problem you can solve, your name and number are right there stuck to the page for them to contact you.

35.   Categories of customers

Categorize your customers into different groups. The criteria to include are profitability; time spent handling orders and special requests. With these categories you can develop a plan to focus much of your time on the most profitable customers.

36.   Marketing – The battle of perceptions

In the battlefield of marketing, perception of your company, brand, product or service wins over everything else. Therefore, it is more important to work on the branding of your company, product or service than on the product itself. Don't get me wrong, your product does have to deliver good value but more time should be spend on marketing the product to increase sales for your business.

37.   Ignore the competition

Sometimes, we are too concerned about our competitors and we forget about everything else. Believe first, with confidence in your vision, don't worry about your competition.

38.   Be tenacious in your vision

The only failure is when you quit. Setbacks are the necessary evils in every business, they aren't failures. Be determined in whatever you are doing by keeping your eye set on your vision.

39.   Tips for magazine advertising

It is proven that a two-page spread attracts about one-quarter more than a one-page ad. A full-page ad attracts one-third more readers than a half-page ad. With regards to illustrations and photos of the product advertised, people tend to respond better to images showing the product in use rather than those that show the product only. Pictures of people in ads attract more attention than those without.

40.   Increase the frequency of ads shown

Often, companies with a limited advertising budget would choose to create larger, more visible ads that restrict them to advertise less frequently. However, a more effective way is to run more frequently with smaller ads even though they may appear less visible. The reason is because most people typically don't respond to ads the first time they see them. Prospects may need to see the ad a number of times before they take action.

41.   Know the deciding factor

People tend to react emotionally when making decisions. However, they like to believe that their decision was made based on rational thinking. So when presenting your offer, a smart marketer will first include the emotional motivator that wins the customer over and also encompass the rationality element to satisfy the customer's need to rationalize.

42.   Observe and learn from business outside your industry

Look outside your industry for the best business examples. It isn't enough for you to only measure yourself against your competition because you'll only be as good as or a little better than they are. However, your customers are experiencing good customer service, quality billing systems in industries outside yours and they are unknowingly pitting your company delivery against those benchmarks as well.

43.   Working the "willing suspension of disbelief"

People are choosing to buy from other people rather than from faceless corporations. Even though these people might not exist, having a human face for the company beats having just a company brand name.

44.   Use the upper left

Eye maps have shown that the first thing you look when reading an article, catalogue or any reading material online or offline for that matter, your eye will rest first at the upper left hand corner of the spread. That's the place you can place your best seller. If your best seller is not an eye catching product or service, use an eye catching visual on the upper left and direct your reader to your actual ad elsewhere on the spread.

45.   Speed up the loading of your web page

The most frequently cited reason for leaving a particular site is the slow downloading time. Hence a faster loading of your site may potentially increase your product or service being seen.

46.   Frequently update your site

Update your site weekly or if possible daily so that traffic will continue flowing to your site. People return as repeated visitors to a site because of new information.

47.   Associate with holidays and Special Occasions

Adapt your website page to reflect what's going on in the world. On special holidays or occasions such as Christmas time, decorate your web site just like you would decorate your own storefront.

Donna Nelson

48.   Respect your customers' time

Try as much as possible to start off with emailing your customer. When that doesn't get you a response, send a fax over. If that also doesn't work, give them a call. However, use this as the last resort because customers are busy too and their time is valuable. Be patient and wait for their responses.

49.   Motto

A catchy slogan or motto can be a powerful advertising message. "When you care enough to send the very best" – Hallmark has used this motto for years and it has made sending Hallmark cards a measure of how important the card recipient is.

50.   Sponsorship

Your company can provide sponsorships to various groups to get involved in the community. One example is to sponsor a local sports team. Your customer base can be increased by people related to the sports team, i.e. family and friends of the players. Furthermore, your company name and brand can be actively promoted by being printed on the jerseys, collaterals etc. of the sports team.

CHAPTER 5- WHY A BEGINNER LIKE YOU SHOULD OUTSOURCE

Outsourcing wasn't in vogue until a few years back. In fact, people even thought it quite embarrassing to tell someone that they were outsourcing their work. The general impression was that they weren't up to the task and the unspoken belief was that outsourced work would always be of an inferior quality.

But times have changed. Today, not only has outsourcing become very popular but it has also practically become the norm for businesses. With the grand popularity that home businesses have achieved, the acceptability of outsourcing has reached its zenith as well.

How could a single person working from home carry out all tasks related to a business without depending on a freelancing professional whom they can outsource their work to?

Here are the top reasons why you must consider outsourcing your business:-

- You can take up more work from a better range of clients because you have an army of people working with you.

- You can get diversity in your team. When you find different outsourcing professionals, you find that these people are of different qualifications and skill-sets, which means that you can even take up work which you were initially avoiding because of your own limitations.

- You cannot handle all of the tasks related with a business alone. There will be several things you are not very conversant with and things that you don't like doing. If that is the case, you might find outsourcing to be a great option to accomplish these tasks adequately.

- Outsourcing definitely helps you meet deadlines better.

- For some people, outsourcing is also a means of reducing costs. If a particular service is expensive in your part of the world, you could find a professional from another part of the world where that particular service is cheaper. A lot of people outsource work from the developed countries to the developing countries where the economic equation helps them reap better savings and stay within tighter budgets.

Most importantly, when you work from home, you might find yourself to be quite lonely, especially when you have to make important decisions. However, when you have intelligent professionals on your team, you do find this task easier.

What Areas of Business Can You Outsource?

Any business – whether it is a home business or a large corporate venture – entails a lot of things. With a large business, it is quite easy to see that there is much involved, but even with home businesses there are various processes, such as planning, finding work, execution of various tasks, communication, payment handling and accounting and further investments. If you are planning to be a home business entrepreneur, you can see that there are various things for you to do. So, which of these can you outsource?

With the Internet making the whole world such a closely-knit domain, you can find professionals to handle all kinds of tasks. They will even plan a whole business venture for you if you have the funds. However, at least initially, you will be on a budget and it will be better to outsource only the things that you really cannot do.

The best idea is to outsource some of the execution aspect of your business. For example, if your home business is about handling content writing jobs, you could outsource the actual writing part. Nevertheless, the things that are integral for keeping your business going such as planning, obtaining work, communicating with clients, payment handling, etc. should be done by yourself. A lot of people obtain work for higher sums of money and pay a flat rate to writers whom they outsource the work to, keeping the difference as their earnings.

It really helps when you outsource the execution part of your work because of various reasons.

• The execution part is always the most laborious task. If you are running a website design and Development Company, the actual designing of the website is the most difficult thing. If this aspect were outsourced, you could focus on getting more clients, while at the same time you are getting the jobs done as well.

• Also, you can control the execution part better. When some content is written by your employee, you could check its quality and send it back for proof reading or editing if required. When someone designs a logo for your client, you could review it and suggest changes. Overall, you can supervise everything.

When your business grows, you will find that you need to outsource many more things. You might need someone for data entry just to maintain the records of your business or you may need someone just to communicate with your various clients and keep them updated with what's happening. You might need someone to handle the bidding or other routes in which you obtain work or you might even need a virtual manager to handle all these aspects of your business at once.

It is possible to find outsourcing professionals for all your needs, from telemarketing to the complete management of your business. The main thing is in knowing when to use these professionals.

Where Can You Find Virtual but Reliable Team Players?

The best place to get outsourcing professionals is the online jobsites. You will find various categories here known as job categories. When you have a particular work requirement, all you do is post your project in the relevant job category and people who are interested in accomplishing the task for you will make their bids on it. The concept is quite simple, and because only people who are genuinely looking for work can be found on these sites, you can be sure that you will get your work done.

Forums

There are several forums on the Internet where people put up their work requirements and other people take them up. There is a bidding game involved here as well, but it is not as rampant as on the freelance jobsites. Projects need to be posted as individual threads and interested people make their bids on them. You can also invite particular people to work on your project.

Social Networking Websites

All social networking websites can be looked upon as a potential source to get professionals to handle various tasks. As there are groups for freelance professionals on these popular sites, you could become a part of these groups and post your projects.

The only problem with social networking sites is that not everyone there is looking for work as this is not the primary reason for joining. Also, there are no systems in place to protect two individuals who work with each other, like you find escrow systems on freelance jobsites.

Since the online jobsites are the best places for you to get professionals, let us look at them in a little more detail.

- People you will find on the jobsites have registered there with the express intention of finding work. Many jobsites are free to join, but some require paid memberships. Being a paid member may reflect a bit more on their sincerity about being professional.

Hence, you can be sure you get some sincere people to give your work to.

- There are various ways in which you can find how good a particular worker is. Every jobsite has a rating and review system (for the employee as well as the employer) and this helps you decide.

- All websites have an escrow system. This takes care of all disputes. Once an escrow is made, the website will arbitrate any problems that arise.

- You can make detailed project posts, outlining clearly what you want to be done and the budget you can afford. People make bids accordingly, so you can be sure you won't have to bargain.

- You can ask people to show samples of their past work.

- You can invite people to bid on your project.

It is very simple to post projects on online jobsites. Many of them, like GetAFreelancer, allow you to post projects for free (though they do take a $5 refundable deposit for each project you post). You only have to post all details of the work as you want it, spell out the timeframe and the budget you can offer and post it in the relevant category. Your project becomes live instantaneously and people start bidding. All you have to do is look at the bids closely and make your decision on whom to select for your job.

You cannot communicate personally with the bidders until you select them. However, there is a private message board that helps you communicate with them, subject to certain restrictions (for example, you cannot give out your personal contact details in any way). This helps you decide better about whom to select.

Many people are forging fruitful and long-term work relationships through these online freelance jobsites, irrespective of geographical barriers. Without the hassle of actually needing employees on their premises, they are able to get their work done professionally and, in most cases, at low cost.

Choosing the Right Outsourced Employees for the Job

When you select your outsourcing professional from a freelance jobsite like GetAFreelancer, ScriptLance or oDesk, there are several ways in which you can make sure you are selecting the right person.

Firstly, you have to ensure that your project details are quite clear. These are the things your project post should cover:

• The nature of your work

• The amount of work in total

• Any milestones, i.e. if you want the work to be completed in small chunks and within what time frame

• The time you can give for the completion of the whole project

• The price you are willing to pay

• Any special qualifications you are looking for in your employees

• Any characteristics that you don't want in your employees

• Special points that you will need to make your decision, such as samples.

Donna Nelson

Most importantly, make sure that you post the project in the right category. People will get alerts only based on the categories they have applied for.

When you take care to spell out as many details as you can, you can be almost sure that you will get the right people bidding on your work. You may only get a few bids, but they will be quality ones.

Make sure to check out all the samples of their work because this is your most important judging point. If you want an original sample, you can mention that in your project post itself and people who are willing to give you an original sample of their work will do so.

In any case, it is a good idea to only post a short-term project initially until you build a trust factor with an employee. Once that is set up, you can go for longer term projects.

Choose people for the following qualifications:

• The quality of their work, which you can see through their samples.

• The ratings and reviews they have obtained on the site.

• Their responsiveness – it is very important they respond to your emails quickly and it's best if they have an instant messaging ID that they can use.

• Their pricing – price shouldn't be an important factor unless you are working on a budget.

Once you get a good professional, make sure you pay them promptly and give them a review according to their work. This ensures they will stay with you longer and you won't have to undergo the hassle of repeatedly looking for employees.

CHAPTER 6- A FAIR EMPLOYER PAYS WELL

In any business association, money is of paramount importance so it is imperative that you have the money equation set right. The beauty of looking for outsourcing professionals on the Internet is that you can benefit from a very wide range of budgets. Since it is people who are going to bid on your projects, you can select them according to what you can pay. You initially set a ballpark figure of what you can pay and most people will bid within this range. Whatever your budget is, you will be able to find good professionals to work for you within that range. Remember that you are looking at the global marketplace here, and people in other countries may work for much less or much higher than what they do for in your local area.

Different jobs have different money equations. It is quite all right if you bid a low budget project initially just to get the feel of the professional's work. You can tell them that you will review payments after you have seen their work. This works well and it also keeps the professional motivated because of the better payments that are poised to come their way.

When you are posting your project on a jobsite, do take some time to check out similar projects that are posted by other people. This will give you a good idea of what you should pay. But, more importantly, you must keep your own budget in focus when posting the project.

Escrows

Escrows help the employer as well as the employee in an outsourcing equation. We shall learn more about escrows in the next chapter.

Online Banks

PayPal is the most popular online bank used by freelance outsourcers. It is followed (though not closely) by Moneybookers. If you are going to outsource a lot, it is also a good idea to have a Payoneer debit card since it is affiliated with most of the freelance jobsites including GetAFreelancer, ScriptLance and oDesk. Releasing money from these sites to this debit card does not attract any fees either.

If you want to get the best people working for you, you simply cannot ignore milestones and escrows. Milestones are especially important when you are working on huge projects and want people to give you their deliverables in smaller installments so that you could manage work at your end as well. And we have already seen how escrows are important.

Some websites, like eLance in particular, help you to state the form in which you want your deliverables. You could actually set up milestones for the whole project. Among other benefits, this ensures that your employee can manage the deadline in a much better manner. You can also keep tabs on things better.

It is ideal anyway to post only short-term projects at the start, until you have a rapport set up with the worker. Even though everything might seem all right to you in the bid, there are chances that something might go wrong when the actual project is underway. If you have a long project running, it could be cumbersome to bail out of these difficult situations. However, a short-term project can help.

On GetAFreelancer, the shortest project you can post should be worth $30. However, on most other sites, there is no minimum limit for the project you post.

The best way to make the payment is through an escrow system. Most jobsites work with escrows (which is actually the main reason why you should use these freelance jobsites because an escrow protects both parties). When you select a bidder, you deposit some money into an escrow account. This money is held by the website but not released to the bidder yet. When they accomplish the task, you can direct the website to release the funds to them.

Escrow helps you because if there is any problem with the project later on and you don't feel like you should pay, you could ask the website to arbitrate. No freelance website will arbitrate if an escrow wasn't made. Also, the worker knows that you have money for the project and it motivates them to do a better job.

ABOUT THE AUTHOR

Donna Nelson didn't grow up wanting to be a business consultant and entrepreneur. Her dream was actually to become a surgeon, much like her father. However, destiny seems to have other plans for her as she was drawn into the intricate world of business financing and the other elements that make a business successful.

Today, Donna coaches entrepreneurs to get their sales up. She also offers consulting pro bono to struggling businesses on the verge of bankruptcy.

www.ingramcontent.com/pod-product-compliance
Lightning Source LLC
Chambersburg PA
CBHW051254170526
45165CB00004B/1709